This book is on loan from
Library Services for Schools
**www.cumbria.gov.uk/**
**libraries/schoolslibserv**

**County Council**

A city adventure in ...

# New Delhi

by Amy Allatson

Words in yellow can be found in the glossary on page 24.

# Contents

Page 4    What is a City?

Page 6    Where is New Delhi?

Page 8    Where and Why?

Page 10    Sightseeing in New Delhi

Page 12    Food in New Delhi

Page 14    Travelling Around New Delhi

Page 16    Where do People Live in New Delhi?

Page 18    Geography

Page 20    Out and About

Page 22    What is It?

Page 23    Quick Quiz

Page 24    Glossary and Index

©2017
Book Life
King's Lynn
Norfolk PE30 4LS

**ISBN:** 978-1-78637-051-8

**Written by:**
Amy Allatson

**Edited by:**
Charlie Ogden

**Designed by:**
Natalie Carr

# What is a City?

Cities are urban settlements. They are bigger in size than towns and villages and have larger populations. Cities are usually very busy places with lots of buildings.

In every country there are cities and most countries have a capital city. Cities are often home to people from many different cultures.

WHAT IS A CAPITAL CITY?
A capital city is usually home to a country's government.

859912

5

# Where is New Delhi?

New Delhi is one of the busiest cities in the world. It is located in the north of India.

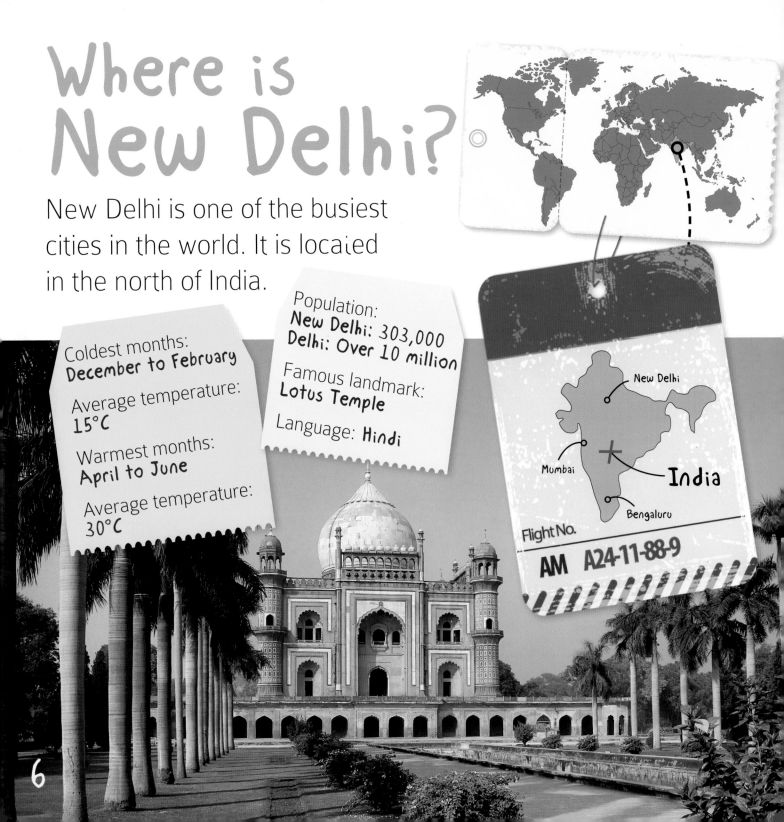

Coldest months:
**December to February**

Average temperature:
**15°C**

Warmest months:
**April to June**

Average temperature:
**30°C**

Population:
**New Delhi: 303,000**
**Delhi: Over 10 million**

Famous landmark:
**Lotus Temple**

Language: **Hindi**

New Delhi

Mumbai

India

Bengaluru

Flight No.

AM  A24-11-88-9

Delhi

New Delhi

New Delhi is the capital city of India. New Delhi is a small area in the much larger city of Delhi.

# Where and Why?

India Gate

The land that New Delhi is built upon has been home to people for thousands of years. There are many ancient landmarks that were built by the different leaders that have ruled over the city.

The capital city of India used to be Kolkata, which is located in the east of India. Over 100 years ago, Britain moved India's capital city to New Delhi.

India

New Delhi

Kolkata

Flight No.

AM A24-11-88-9

9

# Sightseeing in New Delhi

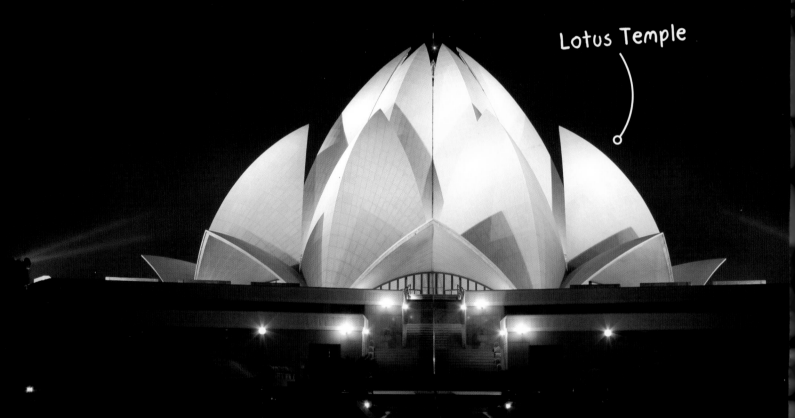

Lotus Temple

There are lots of things to do and see in New Delhi. **Tourists** can visit the famous Lotus Temple, which is a place of **worship** built in the shape of a lotus flower.

Tourists can also visit the Red Fort. The Red Fort was home to the leaders that used to rule over New Delhi.

# Food in New Delhi

Food in New Delhi is often very colourful and full of spices. Butter chicken is a dish made from chicken cooked in butter. It is usually served in a spiced curry sauce.

Curries are usually served with rice.

126685

Street food is very popular in New Delhi; there are many markets and stalls in the city where people can buy food.

# Travelling
## Around New Delhi

People can travel around New Delhi in an auto-rickshaw. An auto-rickshaw is a three-wheeled taxi that many people use to travel around the city more quickly.

Auto-Rickshaw

People can also travel around the city by bus or by car.
The roads are usually very busy so it can often take a long
time to travel somewhere.

# Where do People Live in New Delhi?

Poor people in New Delhi live in overcrowded, dirty areas called slums. They make their homes out of cardboard or other materials they can find.

Over half of India's population lives in slums.

Families in India usually live together with grandparents, parents and children all living in the same house.

# Geography

The River Yamuna runs through Delhi and flows into the River Ganges.

The River Ganges, Varanasi

The weather in New Delhi changes throughout the year. From July to September it is very hot and there is a lot of rain. This is called the monsoon season.

# Out and About

People can visit one of New Delhi's many street markets. The biggest is called Chandni Chowk and people can buy many spices and interesting souvenirs there.

Chandni Chowk Market

Lodi Gardens

People can also visit the city's biggest park, which is called the Lodi Gardens. The park has lots of flowers, trees and ancient landmarks.

# What is It?

Can you write down what's in the pictures below?

These all things that are found in New Delhi.

# Quick Quiz

1. How many people live in New Delhi?

2. Which dish comes from New Delhi?

3. How can people travel around New Delhi?

4. What river flows through New Delhi?

5. What is the largest market in New Delhi called?

# Glossary

| | |
|---|---|
| ancient landmarks | very old and important buildings |
| cultures | attitudes and beliefs of a country or a group of people |
| government | a group of people who make a country's rules and laws |
| populations | the number of people who live in certain places |
| souvenirs | items that are bought on holiday to remember a place |
| spices | ingredients used to add flavour to food |
| tourists | people who are away from home because they are on holiday |
| urban settlements | a place where lots of people live and work, like a town or city |
| worship | a religious act, such as praying |

# Index

Delhi 7-8, 18

food 12-13

Lotus Temple 6, 10

markets 13, 20

parks 21

population 4, 16

Red Fort 11

River Ganges 18

settlements 4

spices 12, 20

tourists 10-11

travelling 14-15

## Photo Credits

Abbreviations: l-left, r-right, b-bottom, t-top, c-centre, m-middle.
Front Cover - Dja65. 2-3 Boris Stroujko. 4 - CroMary. 5 - Zarya Maxim Alexandrovich. 6 - Don Mammoser. 7 - Mikadun. 8 - Mukul Banerjee. 9 - Radiokafka. 10 - paul prescott. 11 - szefei. 12 - Ronald Sumners. 13m- Silentgunman. 13tr - Silentgunman. 14 - Yavuz Sariyildiz. 15 - zeber. 16 - Dmitry Zimin. 17 - Shanti Hesse. 18 - Alenq. 19 - Donald Yip. 20 - saiko3p. 21 - Pikoso.kz.
Images are courtesy of Shutterstock.com. With thanks to Getty Images, Thinkstock Photo and iStockphoto.